The Cornish pasty £65 million to the That's around 3% gross domestic pr

C000064491

It has been an honour to research and write this book. And whilst there are many people I have to thank, above all I have to thank the pasty. Its rich heritage and passionate modern-day purveyors have made this dish a timeless and exceptionally mighty meal.

Rolled up inside the pasty's delicious meat and vegetable filling is a story that's marinated over centuries and today, marries both the old and the new.

The traditional recipe for a Cornish pasty, which has just won an E.U. Protected Geographical Indication status, is hundreds of years old. It has sustained even more Cornish households and small businesses on its journey through time.

Today, the pasty's success is very much down to the work of Cornwall's local and artisan bakers, a few family confectioners and a handful of large-scale pasty producers.

The 'girt bigguns' in the pasty world are some of Cornwall's largest employers, all of whom have helmed their companies through the turbulent seas of Cornwall's economic down turn and the more recent (and more uplifting) Objective One rural regeneration programme.

Whatever shape or size, almost all of Cornwall's pasty-making businesses have been born from a traditional family recipe. One that, over many generations, has been handed down and honed to perfection into the very hand held parcels we enjoy today.

Generations of Cornish butchers, bakers, farmers and food producers have been the 'behind the scenes' power that's very proudly positioned the pasty on the shelves of supermarkets, filling stations and corner shops across Great Britain.

It's easy to judge the big boys. Those, whose hundreds of workers fill pasties in their thousands every day, but they've provided full time employment and kept vital links in the supply chain connected as Cornwall has undergone unstable times and economic uncertainty.

Today, their considerable efforts to plough back profits into projects like this, as well as sporting events, agriculture and local sourcing programmes, reflect an ongoing commitment to the pasty recipe. One that, because of their efforts and the most recent P.G.I. award, will go on to sustain future generations of families in Cornwall.

"How on earth can there be a *Little* Book of the Pasty. Is it full of those recipes of which only one is right??? And that of course is mine!!"

Fi Collett of Lerryn.

When you bite from a pasty
from Cornwall,

Know it's a story of the old and
the new,

Sup on its savoury, let it melt in
your mouth,

But know only Cornwall makes
a pasty that's true.

The Cornish Pasty Association (CPA) began in 2002 and set out to champion and protect the quality and reputation of the Cornish pasty. Today it has over 50 different members.

On the 20th August 2010, the world's largest Cornish pasty was baked by The Proper Cornish Food Company as part of the festivities for Fowey Regatta Week.

The winning pasty contained 1,750,000 calories, measured over 4 metres and weighed 850 kilos. The pasty was baked in a custom built oven and took over 11 hours to cook.

When The Proper Cornish Food Company attempted their world record-breaking attempt, the pasty they made was so big it had to be transported, while cooking, to a special weighbridge.

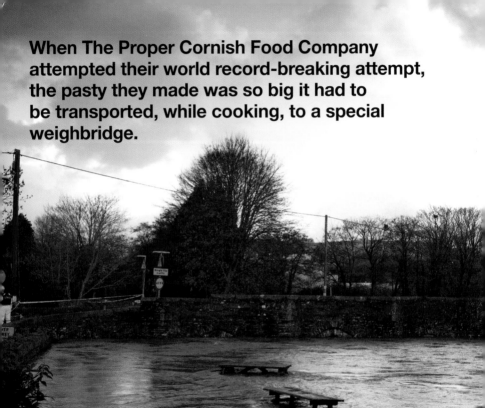

Runners up, Lostwithiel Bakery, held a peeling party the night before the event and peeled their way through 4 sacks of potatoes, 4 sacks of Swedes and the same in onions (now that really is something to cry about).

Sadly, later that year, real tears were shed as Lostwithiel Bakery was hit by the November floods. Barry Green, owner of Lostwithiel Bakery, was working as the River Fowey burst its banks. He recalled that "one minute he was baking, the next he was up to his waist in muddy water... the shop was pretty much destroyed".

PASTY DAY

for Morvah Church and The Community

TUESDAY 3rd AUGUST 11am

car boot . raffle . pasty shy . stalls . mini assault course . bouncy castle

MUSIC
ON THE GREEN
PASTIES, TEA and
HOMEMADE CAKES
IN THE CHURCH

EVENING BBQ &
BAR WITH MUSIC
IN THE MARQUEE
Details:
01736 787 808
www.morvah.com

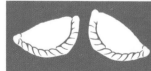

Every first Tuesday in August, the folk of St Morvah celebrate St Morvah Pasty Day. With just 79 villagers, St Morvah is one of the smallest parishes in Cornwall.

The tiny community can be found in West Cornwall, on the magnificent coastal road between St Ives and St Just.

In Crantock, near Newquay, St Carantoc is heralded the patron saint of the pasty and every year on the 16th of May local people hold a church service and feast week in his honour.

Saint Carantoc was a 6th century abbot and confessor who lived in Wales, Ireland and Cornwall. The village of Crantock and its church are named after him.

The word 'oggi' or 'oggy' is sometimes used to describe a pasty, but beware its limitations!

'Oggi' comes from the word 'hoggan' - a dish of pork wrapped in unleavened barley bread. The term was also used to describe a miner's bag.

A 'windy' pasty would be made from left over pastry, rolled out into a round, folded, then crimped and baked. Once cooked it would be opened, coated in **a layer of jam** (and scoffed while warm - yum).

A 'rounder' is a round pasty, all the same ingredients just double the size! A rounder was often served on special occasions or as a Sunday lunch.

In excess of 106 million pasties leave Cornwall every single year.

That's nearly 2 million a week, it's our largest and most famous export.

If you lined them all up end-to-end; that's enough pasties to get from Newquay Airport to Auckland and back or 18 trips from Lands End to John O'Groats...

...or twice around the moon!

The word 'tiddly' was an old naval term for 'proper' so the term 'tiddly oggie' translates to 'proper pasty'.

The word 'tiddy' is a local term for potato. In some corners of Cornwall, a 'tiddy oggie' would have described a pasty filled with just that - tatties.

In May 2008, chefs at Kingsley Village, Fraddon, created a pasty recipe using grey squirrel meat (they must have been nuts!).

However, centuries ago, the pasty would have been filled with just about anything and eaten just about anywhere - except at sea.

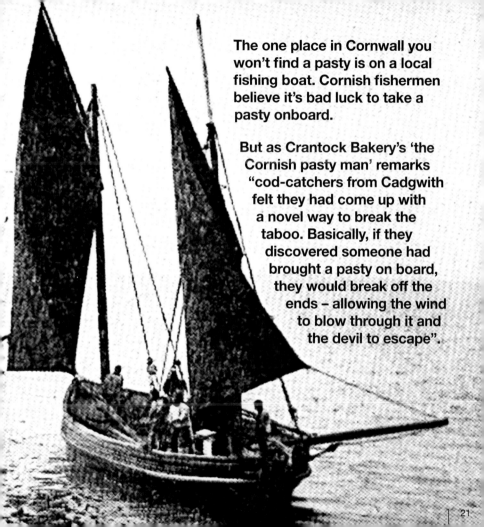

The one place in Cornwall you won't find a pasty is on a local fishing boat. Cornish fishermen believe it's bad luck to take a pasty onboard.

But as Crantock Bakery's 'the Cornish pasty man' remarks "cod-catchers from Cadgwith felt they had come up with a novel way to break the taboo. Basically, if they discovered someone had brought a pasty on board, they would break off the ends – allowing the wind to blow through it and the devil to escape".

ENTIRELY FREE
EMIGRATION
TO
VAN DIEMEN'S LAND
AND
New South Wales.

Mr. LATIMER,
OF TRURO,

Is desirous of obtaining, IMMEDIATELY, a LARGE NUMBER of Emigrants belonging to the class of *Mechanics*, Handicraftsmen, *Agricultural Laborers*, Carpenters, Quarrymen, Masons, and Domestic Servants.

The Emigrants must consist principally of married couples. Single women, with their relatives, are eligible, and in certain cases, *single men*.

The age of persons accepted as Adults is to be not less than 14, nor, generally speaking, more than 35 ; but the latter rule will be relaxed in favour of the parents of children of a working age.

The Colony of Van Diemen's Land has been established more than half-a-century, and possesses the usual advantages belonging to the Australian Settlements. It is not subject to drought, and affords a peculiar demand for the classes above-named.

No CHARGE for CHILDREN!!!

Applications, *post-paid*, or personal, to be made to Mr. LATIMER, 5 Parade, Truro.

E. HEARD, PRINTER AND BOOKBINDER, BOSCAWEN-STREET, TRURO.

Today, the pasty is a world famous dish. It was first exported during the 19th century by tin miners who left Cornwall to find work in South America, New Zealand, Australia and Mexico.

During the 1800s, in some parts of America, the pasty was called a 'Cousin Jack's mouth organ'. During the great emigration, 'Cousin Jack' became the term which described a Cornishman abroad.

Between 1861 and 1900, 45% of men between the ages of 15 and 24 left Cornwall for the New World. A further 30% left for other parts of Great Britain. Today, over 4 million people arrive in Cornwall to have a holiday every year (and a few of our pasties. When the visitors arrive, the local consumption of pasties doubles).

Ever heard the West Cornwall phrase

'cut your hand have 'ee?'

It's an old saying used when someone sees another person taking a bite from a pasty from someone else's hands.

The West Cornwall Pasty Company began in 1998. Its founders, a couple of surfers Gavin and Aaron and their dad, Ken Cocking, were based in Cornwall and built the business with an original budget of £2,000.

The firm struggled to begin with, forcing the family to sleep on the basement floor of one of their shops in order to save money but just 10 years on and an additional investment of £40,000, the family and shareholders sold their business for over £40 million.

Today, the West Cornwall Pasty Company has over 70 outlets across the UK and employs over 500 staff. Across its numerous shops and kiosks, during peak pasty purchasing periods, the company sells over 160,000 pasties a week, that's over 8 million pasties a year and they are all handmade in Cornwall (hooray!).

"The Cornish pasty is, and has been from time immemorial, the staple dish of the County... in its various forms [the pasty] is delectable, dainty and deservedly world famous" Edith Martin, The Cornish Recipe Book.

"There are pasties and there are Cornish pasties."

Valerie Elliot, The Times.

"In its traditional form, the Cornish pasty is symbol, sustenance and speciality" Mary Wright, Cornish Treats.

The pasty is without doubt Cornwall's signature dish, it's a national emblem and has a rightful place alongside the banner of St Piran, Cornish tartan, Trelawney and the Cornish Chough.

Whenever Cornish teams are playing away at national events the pasty goes with them and you can't walk more than 100 yards down any Cornish street without passing a butcher, baker or specialist pasty shop that will sell you one.

The Cornish are mad about pasties, down here folk are extremely proud of the history of the dish and are particularly passionate about how they are prepared and cooked. When I was approached by the Cornish Pasty Association to research and write a book about this mighty all-in-one meal, it was a great honour.

I'd be lying if I didn't share that I gulped a number of times (and a number of pasties) at the thought of this project. There are already some wonderfully written books that cover the subject more than adequately and I can't bake for toffee.

Most of all, this is the one dish in Cornwall that everyone, and I mean everyone, has a stake in (if you can pardon the pun). **So, just like the pasty recipe, there was a lot to get right.**

As a researcher and writer, it seems to me that the trouble, yet overwhelming triumph, of the pasty is the fact that everyone who lives or has a connection to Cornwall has something to share or say about the dish. Ask the question "what should a proper pasty look and taste like?" and you're in for a lengthy debate.

Everyone in Cornwall has an opinion on who makes the best pasty and for most, it seems, the benchmark for the ultimate pasty experience is to have one 'just like mother made'. And when that phrase is spoken with a proper Cornish accent, you not only believe it but can almost smell, if not taste, the very pasty made by the particular mother in question.

The Cornish are fanatical about the way a pasty should be prepared, the ingredients that should be used, what it should look like and how it should be cooked. Without exception, every single person I spoke to while collating this book shared a sense of pride in their pasty making process and very much treasured the recipe they use.

Many gave me stories, many shared memories and most talked of family traditions that, just like a pasty's pastry casing, have wrapped themselves around and oozed into the ingredients that go into this extraordinary pastry parcel.

To my mind, there is no doubt whatsoever that the pasty has been the cornerstone of domestic life and household husbandry in Cornwall for well over 300 years. Whilst the very first pasties were probably more tatties than steak and wrapped in jaw breaking barley bread (or early Tupperware as Janet, one of the guides at Geevor tin mine put it). This kind of a meal sustained Cornwall's miners, agricultural workers and not so well off families for centuries.

Just like a pasty, I've tried to fill this book with nothing but wholesome goodness and have attempted to reflect the extraordinary diversity and cultural heritage that surrounds this ancient meal.

It is my hope that just like a pasty, this book is hearty, warm and filling. A thoroughly digestible account of Cornwall and this incredible meal.

(And if I haven't got all the ingredients right, I am in absolutely no doubt that the Cornish will put me right - please get in touch if I've missed a bit or two: emma_mansfield@tiscali.co.uk).

According to ancient manuscripts the pasty is over 900 years old (wouldn't want to eat one that old though).

The earliest reference to dates back to 1170AD and the romantic tales of French writer Chretien De Troyer, set in Cornwall, who alludes to the pasty in some of his stories about the Knights of the Round Table and the legendary King Arthur.

The word 'pasty' originates from the 13th century French word 'pastee' or 'pastez', the French term then became the middle English word 'paste' meaning 'made of pastry'.

Now, because the design of a pasty very simply and beautifully boils down (well bakes to be exact) to a pastry parcel wrapping a filling of meat and vegetables, the exact geographical origins of this very practical dish are hard to pin down.

Nevertheless, the pasty has had some seriously famous fans over the centuries and stars in a number of very famous texts.

Caxton's translations of Geoffrey Chaucer's Canterbury Tales include a reference to the pasty in, quite appropriately, 'The Cooks Tale'.

"Our host answerd and said I grant it thee,
Now tell on Roger look that it be good,
For many a pasty hast thou let blood, l
And many a Jacke of Dover hast thou sold,
That had be twice hot and twice cold."

William Shakespeare refers to the pasty in the 'Merry Wives of Windsor' and 'All's Well That Ends Well'. In Titus Andronicus, the aforementioned character makes a mother eat her two sons, minced as pasty ingredients (nice).

Arguably, Samuel Pepys was the most prolific penpal to the pasty. His diaries include some 46 pasty inspired entries (and quite a few more entered his belly by the sounds of things).

15th June 1664 – "Very merry we were with our pasty, very well baked; and a good dish of roasted chickens; pease, lobsters, strawberries."

6th June 1665 – "But by and by to sleep again, and then rose and to the office, where very busy all the morning, and at noon to dinner with Sir G. Carteret to his house with all our Board, where a good pasty and brave discourse..."

9th June 1665 – "We had a very good venison pasty, this being instead of my stone-feast the last March, and very merry we were, and the more I know the more I like Mr. Honiwood's conversation."

15th August 1665 – "Thence he and I to Sir J. Minnes's by invitation, where Sir W. Batten and my Lady, and my Lord Bruncker, and all of us dined upon a venison pasty and other good meat, but nothing well dressed."

One of the earliest recorded recipes for the pasty dates back to 1392. It can be found in the French book 'Le Menagier De Paris' (The Good Man of Paris).

Le Menagier De Paris is a medieval household book containing all kinds of recipes and cooking instructions. Its pasty recipe suggests a number of fillings, which include venison, chicken, veal, beef and mutton.

The term 'venison' comes from the Latin word 'venari' meaning 'to hunt'.

Centuries ago, the word venison would have described any kind of meat hunted or taken from wild be it duck, boar, pheasant or indeed, deer.

Take A Leg or Fagget of Mutton
(the Bones being taken out) is to
be rubbed over with Cochineal Then
Spice it with, Mace, Cloves, & Allspice,
of Each an Equal Quantity, with Salt
& Pepper; To which Put in A Pint
of Claret or Port in Baking; the —
Crust as Usual. —

14

In Cornwall, the oldest pasty recipe on record dates back 1746. It's kept at the County Records Office in Truro.

The cooking instructions are included in a letter from Jane Barriball of Launceston to a John Tremayne of Heligan, St Ewe. This is what she suggests:

"Take a Leg or Jigget of Mutton (the bones being taken out) is to be rubbed over with Cochineal, then spiced with Mace, Cloves & Allspice, of each an equal quantity, with Salt; a little Pepper. To which put in a pint of Clarret or Port in baking. The Crust as usual".

An abundance of evidence suggests that the pasty has been enjoyed throughout Cornwall and parts of Great Britain and Europe for little short of a millennia. What was originally served up on the tables of the gentry became the staple diet of rural workers in Cornwall (and it still is).

Who owns the intellectual property rights on this ancient dish is hard to say but in Cornwall, the pasty has proudly maintained its place as a packed lunch and plated meal for several hundred years.

As modern cooking methods developed and improved over the Tamar, poverty in Cornwall kept this dish on the table in crib huts, cottages and country homes alike.

In Cornwall, during the 18th and 19th century, agriculture, mining and china clay quarrying consumed more man-hours than any other industry.

Everyone, men, women and children went to work; either out in the fields or in or above largely tin or copper mines. Boys as young as 10 were allowed to work underground whilst the 'Balmaidens', women and young girls, worked above in the mills, sorting the ore.

Whilst Medieval and Tudor recipes took the pasty to the plates of the well to do, 18th century Cornwall took the pasty to work. Across Cornwall's crib and croust huts and down its mines and their mossel holes.

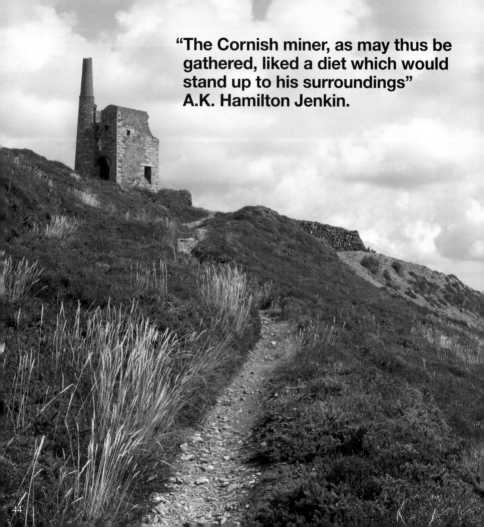

"The Cornish miner, as may thus be gathered, liked a diet which would stand up to his surroundings"
A.K. Hamilton Jenkin.

200 years ago, working hours were long, working conditions poor and as Cornwall's working population increased, food became scarce. Butchers, bakers and millers were rare in Cornwall, domestic ovens scarcer still. At best a rural worker would have cooked a barley-bread pasty in the ashes of their fire or perhaps a cloame oven. In towns, however, a pre-made pastry parcel could be dropped off and cooked at the communal bakehouse for the cost of a shilling a week.

As A.K. Hamilton Jenkin notes in his book 'Cornwall and its People', only the well off could afford meat "labourers would bring their families up with only potatoes and turnips or leeks or pepper grass rolled up in baked barley crust... a long favoured item on the Cornishman's bill of fayre".

"If Cornish food is unwholesome, it none the less managed to sustain a singularly hardy race of men in the past, miners, who walked six miles to work, put in eight hours 'loustering' labouring underground and returned home unspent in the evenings".

As Mary Wright acknowledged; "pasties provided a complete and easily portable meal for miners on long shifts underground".

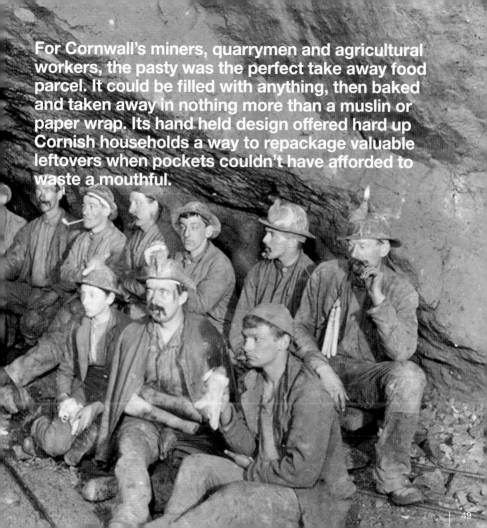

For Cornwall's miners, quarrymen and agricultural workers, the pasty was the perfect take away food parcel. It could be filled with anything, then baked and taken away in nothing more than a muslin or paper wrap. Its hand held design offered hard up Cornish households a way to repackage valuable leftovers when pockets couldn't have afforded to waste a mouthful.

With its pocket sized shape and warm, insulated, shatter-proof case (not to mention its carbo-crammed contents) it's no wonder the pasty became the staple diet for generations of Cornish workers.

"Lets be honest, it was the sandwich of its day, a dish created for the workers lunch break". Anthony Worrall Thompson.

The pasty really was a bright idea.

Just like Humphrey Davey's miner's safety lamp, Goldsworthy Gurney's limelight and Richard Trevithick's steam locomotive - if the pasty hadn't evolved out of necessity, the Cornish would have probably invented it.

During the 18th century, the mines of Cornwall were responsible for producing half of the world's tin supply. At that time Cornwall's mineral industry was the largest enterprise in Europe.

During its hey-day, 19 out of 20 of Cornwall's 19 to 25 year olds would have been working in one of the county's mines. Tens of thousands of people were engaged across the areas mineral industry and most would have had a secondary job as a farm labourer.

Food was an important supply of fuel and warmth so it needed to be substantial and portable and with so many hours being spent at work, meals needed to be quick to prepare and easy to cook.

Starting work at 7am, by midday, clay workers from the mid Cornwall area would have moved up to 20 tonnes of china clay - by hand. After their pasty, they'd walk down the road and do a shift as a potato picker or farm labourer.

After a shift underground, miners would have done the same, especially during the summer months when the fresh water needed to work the top side sorting mills was in scant supply.

53

"I have known instances", wrote Mr Jory Henwood to the Commissioners in 1842, "Where men who had to remain in an atmosphere of 96F [that's 35 degrees celcius] whilst at their employ, at a late hour of the night had to walk three miles to their homes. Some of them were too poor to be well clad, and after so frightful a transition of temperature and so long a walk against a fierce and biting wind, have often reached home without a fire and had to creep to bed with no more nourishing food and drink than barley-bread or potatoes with cold water'.

During the 1800s, the average life expectancy of a Cornish miner was 40 years old. When explosives were introduced, this dropped to 25 years (it's no wonder, if they hadn't been injured underground, other than sleeping, meal times would have been the only time they sat down!).

Meal times in Cornwall were and still are known as 'crib', 'croust' or in West Cornwall 'mossel'. Miners carved mossel holes out of the rock face underground. The mossel room was known as a small dug out that offered protection when firing explosives and a place to eat and drink.

Topside there would have been 'crib' or 'croust' huts and in the china clay area, kettle boys were employed to boil the tea and warm the worker's pasties in crib huts or 'cuddies'.

"If away from the normal eating place, most Cornish folk carried the pasty wrapped in heat retaining cloth. At croust, a miner would remove the pasty and wrap it so he could eat his pasty from the cloth. If his hands were soiled, his pasty did not become so" Harry Tregiglas.

The pasty was also part of the school day; it was carried to class and then baked on the stove.

"At midday you will see bairns running along the street munching great pasties – a Cornish speciality-made with bits of meat and onion and potato with a cover of paste, and the pasty seems to be the school child's usual dinner" G.A.Cooke.

The pasty was portable and powerful. This edible hot water bottle was eaten for lunch and provided enough energy for the entire afternoon and then the long walk home.

The pasty went everywhere, when the Cornish went to work, so did the pasty.

And when work ran out in Cornwall and the miners left for the New World, the pasty, of course, went too.

"[The Pasty's] origins clearly saw it as the ideal meal which a tinner could take down the mine wrapped in a cloth and still find warm three hours later" Colin Luckhurst.

"Wherever in the world there's a hole in the ground at the bottom of it you'll find a Cornishman searching for metal." A.K. Hamilton Jenkin, The Cornish Miner, 1927.

Tin and copper mining, the bulk of Cornwall's mineral trade, reached its peak during the mid 1800s and by 1860, as the industry declined, the great emigration began.

In September 1875, the West Briton reported that over 10,000 Cornish had left Cornwall in the first 6 months of that year. By 1881, Cornwall's population had plummeted by 24% as Cousin Jacks and Jennies headed 'down under'. Between 1815 and 1905, it's estimated that over 250,000 people left Cornwall, that's just under half of our population today.

By 1890, back home, the boom and slump in metal prices had closed all but a handful of mines. In 1905, local papers reported that over £1million was sent back to Cornwall by the 7,000 miners working on the South African Rand alone.

As Cornish miners travelled to work in destinations all over the world, the pasty recipe followed. As the mining frontier of America expanded, the Cornish settled in Pennsylvania, Michigan, Wisconsin, Illinois, Montana, South Dakota, Arizona, Utah, Nevada, California, and Colorado.

"The pasty is a portable beef stew, folded into a purse of a pie dough and baked to a rich golden brown. No one but a cousin Jenny could do a proper job" Angus Murdoch. Cornwall's Legacy to American Mining, Part III, 1970.

Michigan's Upper Peninsular is known as the American centre of pasty-ism. Today, the Pasty Oven is one of the largest pasty producers in the Northern Mid West. The operations director, Susan Gislasen, is a third generation miner and one of the first women to ever work down a Michigan mine. The Pasty Oven supplies over 1,500 outlets and their recipe, a traditional Cornish one, makes the most popular selling pasty in the whole of the United States.

As the Lockwood's acknowledge in their essay in 'The Taste of American Place' the pasty "...is the national dish of Cornwall and it played an important role in the diet of Cornish-Americans wherever they settled....

It was not just a recipe that was passed from one ethnic group to another but an entire cultural complex including occasions for which pasties are prepared, the ways they are prepared and eaten, and some of the folklore associated with them... It is a hearty meal in one... Little wonder that the Finns, Italians and Slavs who saw their Cornish foremen eating a pasty were soon demanding the same of their own wives". (The pasty really did refresh parts other meals didn't reach).

BLASTING

DANGER

~Mining Area~
KEEP OUT

PENALTY $1000
for unauthorised entry
onto mining claims

OPEN S

In Moonta, South Australia, a well known Cornish mining colony, they pride themselves in making some of the finest pasties in the land.

To honour and commemorate the role of the Cornish in Moonta's heritage, every two years the town puts on the largest Cornish festival in the world.

The Kernewek Lowender Festival has been going for nearly 20 years and attracts some 30,000 visitors. The first festival, held in 1973, attracted an unexpected 20,000 people.

During that first weekend, over 15,000 people visited Moonta's mine and museum.

Folk came from far and wide, so much so that the local petrol station ran out of fuel, all of the festival's 8,000 pasties were consumed and the local baker had to sweep the mill floor to get enough flour to cook pasties for the following day.

When Cornish miners left for Mexico's Pachuca, to work for the British Real de Monte mining company, as well as taking their pasty recipes they took their passion for the well known sporting pastime – football (it went on to become Mexico's most favourite sport).

Today, the "pastes" of Real del Monte are made by over 30 local producers and famous throughout Mexico. Whilst the filling is different and the pastry is more of a puff, the design of the dish is very much the same.

In 2008, the state of Hidalgo and Cornwall renewed their connections as the town of Redruth was twinned with Real Del Monte and a Friendship Agreement was signed between Camborne and Pachuca.

In 2009, Pachuca's first ever International Paste Festival took place. Over 8,000 people visited and Cornish pasty demonstrations were taught by Cornwall's Pam Melville from Poldark Mine.

To travel that far and survive that long, the pasty recipe has really proved its staying power.

"Of the five great wonders of the modern world - the telephone, the radio, the television, the motor-car and the Cornish pasty-the most far-reaching must surely be the pasty" Punch Magazine, 1998 Volume 295.

There's no understating that this humble, practical Cornish dish has galvanised communities throughout the world and nowadays it's a cultural icon and valuable commodity.

Back in 20th century Cornwall, the commodity and commercialisation of the pasty was becoming more and more important.

As pasty producers developed their baking businesses so could local suppliers and farmers and the long established relationship between Cornish farmer and Cornish baker began to flourish.

As rail and transportation links improved, Cornwall's tourist industry began to grow and the pasty found a new lease of life.

With just a few mines in operation, the pasty had found its way out of the tunnels, fields and communal bakehouses into the hands of tourists and visitors. Pasty baking was becoming a serious business.

A dish that had endured the hardest of workplaces was now part of the emerging leisure industry in Cornwall.

The pasty's success within the new tourist economy was testament, once more, to its wholesome and sustaining ingredients and wonderful portability. For visitors and holidaymakers, the pasty was the perfect companion for any picnic, painting excursion or big day out on the beach.

And as the tourist industry began to grow, the mining industry collapsed.

Geevor tin mine, St Just, closed in 1986, over 300 local people were made redundant. Whilst it re-opened for a few years, in 1990 the pumps were finally switched off, the mines were flooded and the site abandoned.

As Geevor's assets were stripped and the diggers turned the place over, one of the site's safety managers got in touch with local artist David Kemp.

David Kemp has a workshop in Bottallack, just along from Geevor on the Tinners Coast. The former site manager asked David whether he had any use for an enormous pile of redundant miner's wellies. Kemp salvaged them but wasn't quite sure what for...

A few imaginings and a little while later and the discarded wellies had become the Hounds of Geevor - in David Kemp's own words:

"Relics of a vast subterranean workforce that rarely saw the light of day, each of these hounds fed up to three and a half families (that's 7 pairs of boots per dog!). Released from their underground labours, they were now free to wander the cliff tops looking for a proper job". And as luck would have it they got one.

Cornwall Council, in conjunction with Redruth and Kerrier commissioned David to cast eight of the hounds in bronze. Fittingly, bronze is an alloy of tin and copper, the very commodity that the owners of the boots were excavating from the depths of Cornwall.

Today, the Tinner's Hounds stand very proudly in Tatty Square on Fore Street in Redruth, the once capital of Cornish Tin Mining. Those workingmen's boots are now high street sculptures and a light-hearted tribute to the Cornish miners and something for the grandchildren to cuddle and climb on.

Redruth's South Crofty mine closed in March 1998, it was the last mine to close in the county ending a 3,000 year history of mining in Cornwall.

It was a bleak time for Cornwall; despite the seasonal influx of holidaymakers, the county was experiencing high unemployment, low wages and a very uncertain future.

A year later and Cornwall and Isles of Scilly had been designated as an Objective One area. Objective One was one of three European funding programmes designed to reinvigorate and strengthen the rural economy specifically designated parts of the European Union.

As Cornwall's mineral economy ground to a halt, the pasty making industry began to play an even more crucial role in the wider Cornish economy.

In the 1990s pasty producers were, and still are, an important year round employer (especially in an area where 1/5 of the population are employed via the seasonal tourist industry).

Between 2000 and 2006, EU investment into Cornwall's food sector alone helped create 2,200 jobs, 65 new cheeses and an extra 15 million pasties (no joke… this is the recipe...a recipe for success, I might add).

The Cornish Pasty Recipe
(Makes 15 million!)

The Pastry

1,687,500 kilos of plain flour
862,500 kilos of fat (a mixture of lard and butter)
45,000 kilos of salt.

The Filling

1,687,500 kilos of beef skirt cut into small cubes
15,000,000 large potatoes
375,000 turnips (Swedes).
15 million onions peeled and chopped
Bucket loads of salt and pepper
75,000 litres of water.

Throughout the Objective One Programme, significant investment and time went into reinforcing the links between Cornish baker and Cornish farmer. This was a crucial relationship if growth in the county's food producing sector was going to stay local and become sustainable.

The pasty was becoming a priceless part of Cornwall's regeneration. As pasty makers developed their production lines, they began to diversify adding other pastry items to their product listings. This enabled Cornish bakers and food producers to expand into new, national and wider markets.

Cornish bakers were soon baking for supermarkets and high street outlets all over the UK. By the end of the nineties, it was becoming ever clearer that the pasty was one of Cornwall's most valuable exports.

This revitalising recipe for success needed protection, so in 2002, a group of pasty makers got together to protect their recipe's and the pasty's provenance. The Cornish Pasty Association (CPA) was born.

10 years ago, the CPA set out their aim of protecting the pasty from out of county competitors and to champion its cultural roots in Cornwall. Their focus was promoting and developing a local product with local suppliers.

By 2005, 5,700 tonnes of potatoes, 5,200 tonnes of beef, 310 tonnes of onions and 1,550 tonnes of swede were produced on Cornish farms and ended up in Cornish pasties.

By 2006, and the end of the Objective One Programme, the pasty had become a very precious commodity for Cornwall. So much so, that this traditional and very Cornish recipe for success was starting to attract some stiff competition.

Bakers outside of Cornwall were beginning to jump on the pasty bandwagon but baked a far inferior product. Cornish bakers felt it was necessary to protect their trade and the reputation of their timeless and traditional recipes.

Because of the strong links between pasty producers and local beef and vegetable suppliers, out of county competition presented significant threats further down the supply chain but not for long.

After a great deal of graft and campaigning, in November 2008, DEFRA submitted an application for Protected Geographical Indication (PGI) status to the European Commission on behalf of the Cornish Pasty Association.

The application and the CPA campaign cemented the county's commitment to the pasty. Letters of support came from all corners of Cornwall and beyond.

"I am very ready to help in any way I can with your campaign. I am very happy to eat any number of pasties in public!" **Dr. Caroline Jackson MEP**

"I will of course be delighted to continue my campaign on behalf of genuine Cornish products." **Lord Paul Tyler**

"I congratulate all those involved in maintaining the necessary enthusiasm to achieve PGI status for the Cornish pasty. As you know, I very strongly support this campaign and believe that because of the very strong and well established tradition, it is essential that those pasties which describe themselves as 'Cornish' should only be made in Cornwall." **Andrew George MP**

"I have been a long-term supporter of this application, which is essential to the economic benefit of Cornwall. I have no doubt that the strenuous efforts of so many individuals and organisations will ultimately bear the fruit and will provide the Cornish pasty with the protection it richly deserves and which Cornwall certainly needs." **Colin Breed MP**

In 2011, the status was approved. Today, the PGI puts the pasty up there with Gorgonzola, the Melton Mowbray Pork Pie and Champagne. Commercially, it means that a Cornish pasty can only be named as such if it is made in Cornwall and to a traditional recipe.

Today, the Cornish pasty recipe supports 1,800 workers and a further 13,000 individuals who are employed indirectly.

Annually, the pasty injects a staggering £65 million into the Cornish economy and that figure grows year on year.

So what are vital statistics of a traditional Cornish pasty and what is that traditional recipe?

Well, according to the Cornish Pasty Association...

A genuine Cornish pasty has a distinctive 'D' shape and is crimped on one side, not on the top.

The texture of the filling for the pasty is chunky, made up of uncooked minced or roughly cut chunks of beef (not less than 12.5%), swede, potato and onion and a light peppery seasoning.

The pastry casing is golden in colour, savoury, glazed with milk or egg and robust enough to retain its shape throughout the cooking and cooling process without splitting or cracking.

The whole pasty is slow-baked to ensure that flavours from the raw ingredients are maximised. No artificial flavourings or additives must be used.

And, perhaps most importantly, it must be made in Cornwall.

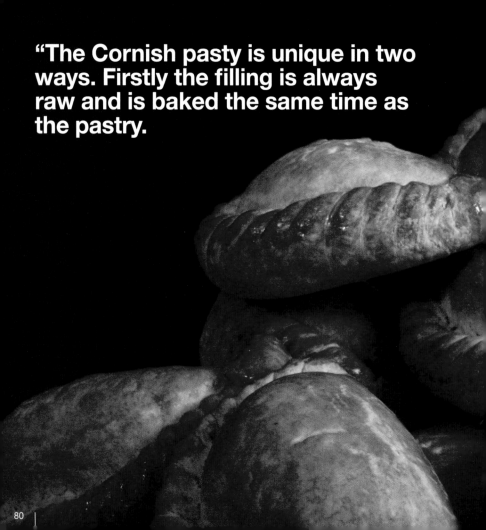

"The Cornish pasty is unique in two ways. Firstly the filling is always raw and is baked the same time as the pastry.

Secondly, it is a meal in
itself. " Hettie Merrick

And as for that recipe...

Well, the pasty recipe can be found in well over 100 different cookery books but most importantly hundreds, if not thousands more, exist in the hearts and minds of generation after generation of Cornish families.

Rather than being committed to paper, pasty recipes have been committed to memory and handed down for over 200 hundred years.

A little book about the pasty would not be complete without a pasty recipe so I asked Elaine Ead, from the Chough Bakery, if I could use the one she has developed for the Cornish Pasty Association.

So...to coin a well known cookery phrase...here's one we made earlier (in Lindsay Bareham's delightful and beautifully written and presented 'Pasties' book there are tonnes more).

The Traditional Cornish Pasty recipe. Makes 4 good-sized ones!

Pastry

500 gms strong bread flour (it's important to use a stronger flour than normal as you need the strength in the gluten for a strong, pliable pastry).
120 gms white shortening
25 gms cake margarine
5 gms salt
175 gms cold water

Mix the fat lightly into flour until it resembles breadcrumbs.

Add water and beat in a food mixer until the pastry clears and becomes elastic. This will take longer than normal pastry but it gives the pastry the strength that is needed to hold the filling and retain a good shape.

Leave to rest for 3 hours in a refrigerator, this is a very important stage as it is almost impossible to roll and shape the pastry when fresh.

The Filling

450 gms good quality beef e.g. skirt
450 gms potato
250 gms swede
200 gms onion
Salt & pepper to taste (2/1 ratio)
Clotted cream or butter (optional)

Chop the ingredients finely then add to the rolled out circles of pastry raw.

Layer the vegetables and meat adding plenty of seasoning.

Put your dollop of cream or a knob of butter on top. Then bring the pastry around and crimp together.

Try practising on a potato first or just flatten like a turnover and mark with a fork.

Handy hints.

Always use a firm waxy potato - Maris Piper or Wilja.
Put in plenty of seasoning.
Ensure that all your veg is freshly prepared.
Never attempt to add carrot, this is sacrilege!!!
Butter or cream gives the pasty that extra richness.

Cooking time and temperature

Gas No 6 for approximately 50 mins -1 hour.
Electric 210 approximately 50 mins -1 hour.
Fan assisted 165 approx 40 mins.

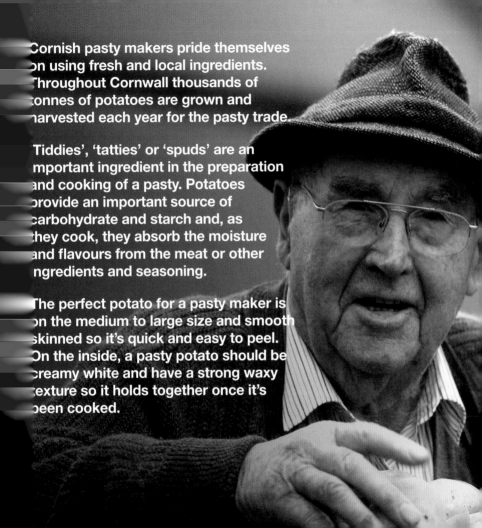

Cornish pasty makers pride themselves on using fresh and local ingredients. Throughout Cornwall thousands of tonnes of potatoes are grown and harvested each year for the pasty trade.

'Tiddies', 'tatties' or 'spuds' are an important ingredient in the preparation and cooking of a pasty. Potatoes provide an important source of carbohydrate and starch and, as they cook, they absorb the moisture and flavours from the meat or other ingredients and seasoning.

The perfect potato for a pasty maker is on the medium to large size and smooth skinned so it's quick and easy to peel. On the inside, a pasty potato should be creamy white and have a strong waxy texture so it holds together once it's been cooked.

Just like the pasty, potatoes have played an important role in Cornwall's agricultural economy. The county's warm, wet climate and good soil conditions make it an excellent place to grow spuds. The milder winter weather enables West Cornwall growers to harvest potatoes that little bit earlier than other parts of the UK, giving them a competitive edge and the capacity to grow a second crop.

The Cornish Early, as it's known, is not a specific potato variety but a term that's used to promote the first lot of potatoes dug and sold out of West Cornwall. Cornish Earlies have become a bit of a delicacy. Their out-of-county commercial value and smaller size makes them too expensive for the pasty trade but 'second earlies' and 'main crop' certainly make the grade.

Some pasty makers like King Edwards, some like Wilja's and others Maris Pipers. The Estima variety, the second most popular potato in terms of planting in the UK, scores very highly as a pasty potato. In Cornwall it's well known for it's creamy flesh and waxy texture.

When is a turnip not a turnip? When it's in a pasty.

Another important ingredient in a pasty is swede... or is it turnip... or is it turmet... or is it Swedish turnip... once and for all just exactly what is it?

Centuries ago, when it came to Cornwall and making a pasty, swede and turnip were one and the same.

Along with the Scots, the Cornish are particularly quirky in calling a swede a turnip (it can get very confusing down the grocers and even more so if you come from Essex and are following a traditional Cornish pasty recipe).

Today's turnips are small, white and have a sharp taste. Swedes are much larger, have an orange flesh a taste that little bit earthier.

Today, with the PGI status, a Cornish pasty can only be called as such if it contains swede. That's brassica napo brassica to be precise.

There's an old saying that the Devil never came to Cornwall because there were saints in every corner and Cornish housewives would put just about anything into one of their pies. Today, the best-selling and most popular filling for a pasty is beef (and apologies for the flesh photography!).

Whether the beef is sliced or diced, for centuries and even today, the best cut of meat for a pasty is skirt or chuck steak. Talk to any butcher in Cornwall and he'll list at least one if not both of the above (some suggest shin but it's not as common or as available as the other two).

Beef skirt is prized for its flavour rather than its tenderness, it's a long flat cut of meat that comes from the 'plate' part of the bullock, that's just behind the front legs, underneath the ribs.

Skirt has an open grain, which makes it great for cooking in a pasty. As the temperature of the oven rises, the skirt meat releases its juices providing a great tasting gravy that cooks the vegetables and keeps the entire dish moist (ooo I can almost taste it).

Chuck steak comes from the shoulder part of the animal; the best cut comes from the rib end rather than the neck. Chuck steak is well suited to slower cooking, it's a well balanced cut in terms of meat verses fat percentage so perfect for braising or slow baking in a pasty (I'm getting hungry now).

"An onion can make people cry but there's never been a vegetable that can make people laugh." Will Rogers.

Onions are the third essential vegetable in a traditional Cornish pasty. Until several years ago it was extremely difficult to grow onions commercially in Cornwall.

However, Cornwall's largest pasty maker, Ginsters' commitment to local sourcing has enabled Hay Farm, near Torpoint, to develop and invest in specialist onion-growing methods and can now supply Ginsters with over 40% of it's onion demand.

Onions make us cry because as we break or cut the skin the cells release a sulphurous acid. Onions contain over 150 phyto-chemicals many of which have important health benefits; eating onion use to help treat scurvy and can help lower cholesterol and blood pressure.

" I recently saw a railway man eating lunch at Truro, a delicious smelling pasty on a piece of paper. He said he ate one everyday, and his wife made them everyday and he'd never had a days illness in his life" Prue Leith.

'Tis said, in some parts of Cornwall, that a pasty's pastry case should be tough enough to sustain being dropped down a mine shaft and remain intact at the bottom (not sure I would have wanted to eat one of those but...)

Judging by the fact that the earliest pasties, or 'hoggans' as they were known, were made of barley-bread; a tough, hard and almost inedible type of bake, it's just possible this could well have been true. Equally 'fuggans'; a solid mass of unleavened bread with pork in the middle, would have been just as tough (wonder what people's teeth were like).

150 years ago, wheat flour would have been extremely expensive for mining families so, along with potatoes, barley flour became their staple.

Although Cornish mills could produce flour, it was very often imported and milling as whole ground (of you can pardon the pun) to a halt during the Second World War. Up until very recently, milling wheat was non-existent in Cornwall so commercial supplies come from as far as Russia and Canada.

As part of their 'Cornish Through and Through' proposition, Ginsters has worked with local farmers to reinstate Cornwall's milling wheat crop. In 2006 they were able to buy 2,800 tonnes of authentic Cornish wheat and today, across 9 different farms, a total of 1,100 acres is devoted to growing wheat for Ginsters (and that means lots of pastry).

Talk to any pasty maker in Cornwall, commercial or otherwise, and they've all got a say on which pastry is best. Some, like Toby Tobin-Dougan, from the St Martins Bakery, do a rough puff. Elaine Ead, at the Chough Bakery, does a short crust. Some add a bit of bread flour and some do a full on flakey.

But whatever the bakers choose today, traditionally, because fat – either butter or lard - would have been expensive, a traditional pasty would have very probably had a short crust crust (yum).

In Cornwall, 'tis often said that miners underground would throw any leftover pieces of pasty to 'the knockers'. Miners were a suspicious bunch and believed that the knockers were relatively benevolent mining spirits or the ghosts of Jewish miners who'd gone before them.

Depending on which part of Cornwall you came from, knockers were also known as knackers or buccas. They were said to inhabit the deepest parts of Cornish mines and could be heard knocking as they worked away in the darkness.

Some believed that knockers were helpful; they'd knock away at the richest lodes and show themselves to miners they liked and for that they needed to be respected. The gesture of leaving food for the knockers became a way of pleasing the spirits and, given the claustrophobic and dangerous conditions, it was also seen as a gift for good luck.

The legend of the knockers died out with Cornwall's mining industry but some still believe they live on, in the miles and miles of un-manned tunnels that exist beneath Cornwall's surface (living off leftover pieces of pasty... well some say that the pasty is a good meal for lifting the spirits!).

No matter what recipe, filling or pastry you choose, the secret of a good pasty, it seems, is held within its crimp.

Some people like a really thick crimp, some like it not so. Some crimp to the side and some on top, it really depends upon where you've been raised and what you were brought up on.

But, with the new PGI in place, to sell your pasty as traditionally Cornish, a side crimp is the one for you... in fact it's the law and here's how to do it...

How to crimp a Cornish pasty (the Crantock Bakery way)...

1. Place the ingredients in the middle of the pastry circle.

2. Dampen the exposed edge with water.

3. Lift half of the pastry over the filling to make a half-moon or D shape.

4. Press the edges of the pastry together to seal them together. Turn the pasty so that the sealed edge is along the top.

5. Starting at the left edge of the pasty, take hold between the left finger and thumb and turn it inwards onto the line of the sealed edge. This is to make sure nothing oozes out of the end.

6. Holding the first fold with the left finger and thumb, turn over the immediately adjacent edge, towards you, using the right finger and thumb.

7. Repeat the process all the way along the edge until the pasty is crimped – there should be between 17 and 21 crimps.

8. When you reach the end of the line, turn the end inwards as in step 5.

"YOU'M WELCOME TO A DISH'A TAY AND A CORNISH PASTY"

It's often been said that the crimped edge on pasty evolved as a kind of handle. The pastry crust was held by miners as they ate their way around the pasty and then discarded the crimp at the end.

On one hand (if you can pardon the pun) an edible handle that could be thrown away afterwards would have saved lives. Miners hands would have been filthy, arsenic was just one of the poisonous substances they were exposed to. Discarding the crimp, along with any toxic chemicals or dirt that may have been on their hands makes perfect sense...but not everyone agrees...

On the other hand, many say that every morsel a miner could have got his hands and mouth around would have been eaten rather than tossed for the knockers. Plenty of archive images show that pasties were wrapped in muslin or paper bags, others show girt great big 'uns being grasped firmly round the middle and being eaten end to end.

Not sure it matters really, handle or not, the crimp gives a pasty its hand-blessed and hand-crafted character.

"The true way to eat a Cornish pasty is to hold it in the hand, and begin to bite it from the opposite end to the initial, so that, should any of it be uneaten, it may be consumed later by its rightful owner. Woe betide anyone who takes another person's 'corner'" Edith Martin.

Years ago, housewives would have personalised a miner's pasty by adding his initials. These would have been either carved into the pasty or added with left over pastry.

Initials were always placed in the corner of a pasty and when eaten, folk would leave the initialled bit till last. That way miners could have their (and only their) 'corner for later'. By adding initials, each pasty could be baked to order and identified once cooked.

Father liked mate and tatie best (that's a meat and potato one)
Mother like turmut and mate (that's a swede and meat one)
Boy Jack want all mate (meat only)
Boy Tom like lickey best (leek only)
An' the maidens edden pertic'lar 'tall (they weren't as fussy!)

But when it comes to particular fillings, mind your P's and carrots... Pasties with peas and/or carrots are sacrilege, they are not traditional and certainly not from Cornwall. Cocktail pasties, the smaller ones were traditionally made for children, they were also a convenient way to use up leftover ingredients.

Now, if you're a true pasty connoisseur you can actually identify the 'handedness' of your pasty's crimper. It's all about knowing your cock from your hens!

Right-handed crimpers make hen pasties and cock pasties are made by us lefties. As you take a closer look, you'll notice the different crimps go in different directions.

Cock pasties are pretty rare because around 85% of pasty crimpers are right handed (there's not many of the others left, right!).

"Pastry rolled out like a plate,
Piled with turmut, tates and mate.
Doubled up and baked like fate,
That's a Cornish Pasty."

In workers' cottages and small dwellings, pasties would have first been baked in cloame ovens, a type of masonry oven built into the fireplace.

Cloam or clome ovens are surrounded by clay to stop them from cracking and were lit with dried gorse. Without a chimney, the smoke would leave through the oven door and flow out via the main chimney. Once up to temperature, the ashes were raked to one side and the oven was ready for baking.

At the same time, most major towns in Cornwall would have had a communal bakehouse so pasties could be dropped off on the way to work to be delivered or collected later.

Wealthier families and certainly the manor houses would have had a Cornish Range. Cornish Ranges, also known as 'The Apparatus' or 'Slab' were made out of cast iron and first manufactured in Redruth during the 1830s. They were also engineered at both the Hayle and St Just Foundry where they remained in production until the beginning of the Second World War.

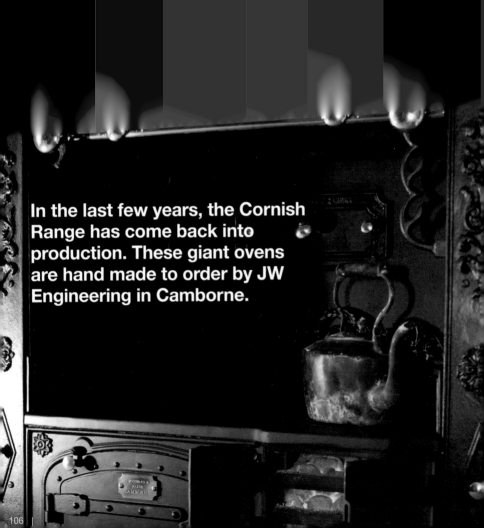

In the last few years, the Cornish Range has come back into production. These giant ovens are hand made to order by JW Engineering in Camborne.

John Woodward, the owner of the business, designs the stoves and subcontracts to the Terrill Brother's Foundry who make the castings from his patterns. All the sheet metal work is produced from LaserMaster in St Day.

The AGA - another popular feature in many of Cornwall's farmhouses - arrived in England in 1929. It was designed by Dr Gustaf Dalén, a blind, Nobel-prize winning Swedish physicist. Dr Dalén wanted to reduce the burden of his wife's domestic duties by creating an oven that was better designed and more economical.

A few years later the AGA was born, but little could Dalén know that in Cornwall the AGA did all those things and cooked great pasties. Furthermore, on countless farms it also saved and still saves the lives of many new born lambs and goslings.

In years gone by, if you dropped by most family run farms first thing or late at night during lambing season, you might just find new-born lambs in the simmering oven of an AGA or Rayburn - not cooking, just gently warming up (honest). Young goslings might also be helped in this way when they needed to be revived or have their down restored when damaged by wet conditions.

Pasty making has always been at the heart of domestic life and in many homes it still is. It's a dish that Cornish men are proud to make and talk about too. Chat to those who've lived in Cornwall for over 25 years or so and they'll share a story about Saturday as pasty day and many a young'un will recall making jam tarts from the left over pastry.

Tamsyn Lewis was taught how to make pasties by her grandpa. Before she was let loose on the real ones, Grampy would give her a little bit of pastry to practise her crimping or carve into family initials. Although Tamsyn's granny was the cook of the house, no one could beat Grampy's pasties - best eaten straight from the oven with a glug of dandelion and burdock.

In the Barker household, your ranking in the family was very much dictated by where your pasty went in the oven. Beware the new boyfriend or son-in-law who'd conveniently drop by in time for dinner on Saturday.

Mrs Barker was no fool, after feeding her grandchildren and 3 daughters, the boyfriend's pasties would always come out next and the boys would compete for who got theirs first! Her husband's was always last out the oven! Hermione, Mrs Barker's granddaughter, had her first pasty to celebrate her first birthday (we start 'em young down here).

In the Barnecut household, it was Mrs Cundy who made pasty making memorable. As a boy, Tom Barnecut remembers Saturdays as pasty days and whilst Mrs Cundy crimped in the kitchen, Tom's job was to polish the silverware. As the pasties baked, he was allowed to make jam tarts with leftover pastry and ever since then the thought of Mrs Cundy's mouth-watering pasties has been synonymous with the smell of silvo, flour and jam!

In the Littleton family, who've farmed in Cornwall for centuries, farmer Gordon Littleton was especially partial to giblet pasty. Meta, his wife would chop liver, gizzard and heart together with shallots and make a cocktail size pasty for Gordon to eat at teatime. The giblets were from the free range, corn fed poultry raised on the farm.

Farmers were, and some still are, renowned for using as much of the animal they killed as possible. Gordon said the only thing he couldn't use from the pig he killed was its squeak. Even the bladder had a use, it was blown up and used as a football - wonder what they did for a rugby ball?

As well as pasty mania, the Cornish are a rugby mad nation too. It's long been a tradition for supporters of the Cornish rugby team to throw a pasty over the posts to bring players good luck in the match.

Legend has it that as pasty sellers drove into town or miner's wives threw pasties down mine shafts, 'oggie, oggie, oggie was the resounding chant. Hungry miners replied Oi Oi Oi. Today, that same chant can be heard along the sidelines of rugby matches across Cornwall and beyond.

The pasty has seen a fair few rugby matches in its time. As an important symbol for Cornwall, along with Cornish kilts, our national anthem, Trelawney and over 10% of the Cornish population, a 4-foot pasty was paraded at Twickenham in 1991. Just before Cornwall won the county championships against Yorkshire.

That day, the Cornish team took 50,000 supporters with them (and probably just as many pasties). The night before, the West Briton newspaper headlined with "last one out, turn off the lights".

Even today, pasty producers get behind many of Cornwall's teams and sporting events. The larger companies take it in turns to sponsor clubs and prizes.

This year, Warren's are looking after the Cornish Pirates and Rowe's sponsor the Redruth team. In gig rowing, Ginsters sponsor the Saltash event and helped the Calstock team buy a brand new pilot gig boat.

Oggy Oggy Oggy!
Oi Oi Oi!
Oggy Oggy Oggy!
Oi Oi Oi!
Oggy!
Oi!
Oggy!
Oi!
Oggy Oggy Oggy!
Oi Oi Oi!

And as pasty power from Cornwall backs more and more sporting and social events, purveyors of pasty associated memorabilia also reap the benefits!

The Cornish Pasty Appreciation Society t-shirt, created by Balcony Shirts, is the 18th best selling t-shirt on the Amazon website (and that's out of a total of 400,000).

These days you can buy pasty shaped earrings, pasty shaped cufflinks, pasty shaped chocolates - even pasty flavour crisps - look out for the Lusty Pirate.

But as tasty as pasty flavoured crisps may be, you just can't beat the taste of a freshly baked pasty. As pasty maker Ann Muller puts it, "every mouthful is a piece of Cornwall - a dream folded heaven".

So who are the people who make our pasty dreams come true? Well, some are individuals who just bake for their locals, some are family bakers who've been going for centuries and some are local firms who've been supplying the nation with a handed down recipe for the last few decades.

Large or small, each pasty maker has an inspirational story to tell. So let start with the girt big 'uns...

Ginsters is the largest pasty maker in Great Britain - probably the world.

If ever there was a company that demonstrates the power of the pasty Ginsters is the one. The company started from a humble, family-run, egg packing business in Callington and today it's arguably the biggest pasty producer on the planet.

The firm traces its history back to the 1960s when owner Geoffrey Ginster had an idea to start a van sales service selling pasties to the locals. The egg packing plant became a bakery and their first order was for 24 pasties, hand crimped by 4 people.

In 1977, the company became part of the Samworth Brothers group and today over 500 people are employed at the Callington site, which produces 3 million savoury pastries a week. They are one of the largest employers in Cornwall.

Ginsters has a 150- strong fleet of vehicles delivering pasties, and other pastry and snack items, to motorway service stations, forecourts and convenience stores throughout Great Britain. It also supplies pasties to all the leading supermarkets. Today, the Ginsters 'Original Cornish Pasty' is the biggest selling savoury chilled product in the UK.

The Callington site uses 50 tonnes of beef a week and has two deliveries of vegetables a day. Sourcing and managing fresh ingredients has been intrinsic to the success of their business and the company has invested significantly in their relationship with local suppliers and farmers.

Over the last few years, Ginsters has worked closely with Cornwall's Agricultural Community so much so that it is now able to source locally grown wheat and onions. Furthermore, 70% of its fresh vegetables and 70% of its fresh beef come directly from Cornish farms.

The Proper Cornish Food Company are based on the edge of Bodmin Moor. They've just been awarded the Guinness Book of Records "World's Largest Cornish Pasty".

Proper Cornish started in 1988, the brainchild of three Cornishmen who were brought up on Cornish pasties. The owners believed that the pasties they bought locally were far inferior to the ones their mothers made. With this in mind, they set out months later to make and sell an authentic, traditional Cornish pasty that tasted just as good as the ones from mum's kitchen.

Over the last 23 years, demand for their pasties has increased exponentially. The company began with a handful of employees, including the mother of two of the shareholders and today they manage over 200 full time staff.

Proper Cornish crimpers make over 50,000 pasties a day. Each one hand made following the same exacting standards as they did when they started out all those years ago.

In 2010, their traditional steak recipe won 'Best Cornish Pasty' at the British Pie Awards.

To this date, the Proper Cornish pasty recipe has never altered nor the care taken in preparing them. All of the vegetables are still purchased locally from farms and farmers in Cornwall and they are prepared in house to ensure the freshest taste.

As well as a producing an award winning traditional pasty, The Proper Cornish Food Company have experimented with some quirkier fillings which include a roast beef dinner pasty, a chicken Balti pasty and a chocolate and banana one! However, the traditional Cornish pasty is still their top seller.

Crantock Bakery started life in the village of Crantock. Their pasty recipe was 'handed down' to one of the villagers and the pasty making business was born!

Sales of pasties grew and grew and soon the bakery had to move to larger premises nearby. In the late nineties, the company moved again to Indian Queens just outside Newquay and this is where it operates today, from a state of the art facility with the highest accreditations.

In 2002, Crantock Bakery was sold to its current owners Nick Ringer and Matthew Hurry and by 2008, the company had been awarded "Bakery Food Manufacturer of the Year."

A few years on and the company employs over 150 people and has the capacity to make up to 140,000 pasties a day, that's around 300 a minute!

Crantock Bakery makes for customers and outlets all over the UK and they export to France, Norway and Cyprus.

The most unusual pasty they've ever made was a special commission from Chatsworth house. The recipe consisted of rabbit, pheasant, vegetables and a rich red wine sauce. However, the favourite is still the "handed down recipe", a traditional steak pasty. Which goes to prove that some old things you just can't beat!

W C Rowe opened his first
Falmouth pasty shop in 1949.

The high street premises had a shop at the front, bakery at the back and living quarters above. Mr. Rowe was known for his perfectionism, all he cared about, other than his fiancée Phyllis Wallis, was how to make the best possible pasty.

Miss Wallis also had an eye for detail and when the couple got married they went into business together, she looked after the displays and front of house while he baked out the back.

The pasty couldn't have found its way into a more passionate and perfectionist pair (well two pairs really) of hands. For over 40 years, the Rowe's lived, breathed and worked pasties and their business went from strength to strength.

Alan Pearce started at Rowe's when he was just 15 years old and took a post as a Saturday boy. In 1975, when the company became limited, Alan was taken on as a director and offered a minority share holding of £8,000.

Mr. and Mrs. Rowe passed away during the 1990s, with no children to inherit their business - they left their shares in the hands of Alan Pearce who then shared the business with his family. Today, the company employs up to 550 people and their new purpose built commercial bakery has the capacity to produce up to 50,000 pasties a day. Rowe's supply pasties to all kinds of different wholesale and retail outlets all over the UK.

Tamar Foods began in 1999. Their first batch of pasties came from the bakery that used to belong to Ginsters.

As Ginsters developed their brand new, purpose-built premises next door, Tamar Foods tapped up new trade supplying pasties and traditional pastry items like pies and sausage rolls, to supermarkets all over Britain.

By 2010, Tamar Foods was producing over 25 million pasties a year, some pasties were bakery made, some were hand crimped and some of their crimpers had a twenty year history of crimping for the company.

In November that same year, Tamar Foods were awarded the prized Best Manufacturer of Prepared Foods - at the Food Manufacturing Excellence Awards (which is the food industry's equivilent to the Oscars). Judges were particularly impressed with Tamar Food's committment and approaches to people development.

Today, Tamar Foods employs over 580 people and sources over 50% of all it's ingredients from the West Country. The company has won a number of awards for it's products and premises and has a number of environmental credentials. Tamar Foods has been a member of the Cornish Pasty Association for a number of years and have represented the association at a number of events including a trip to Number 10 Downing Street.

Elaine Ead, owner of the award winning Chough Bakery, goes to work to one of the best views in Cornwall.

The Chough bakery is slap bang in the middle of Padstow and looks out over the harbour and Camel estuary beyond. Elaine's love affair with the pasty began in 1992; her family used to run the local milk round and when the days of having milk delivered to your doorstep stopped, they decided to turn their premises into a bakery.

Elaines plan was to start baking cakes and bread for locals and holidaymakers but one of her friends suggested success would come if she focused on something else...

"Make a decent pasty and the rest will come".

They were right. 20 years on and Elaine is the face of the Cornish Pasty Association running a small but very successful local business that turns over more than £1million a year.

Although Elaine trained as a cookery teacher, she knew it was important to take local lessons in pasty making, the first of which came from her Cornish mother-in-law. Despite opening the Rayburn to find her first batch of pasties, crimped by her own fair hand, had unfolded in the oven and were 'smiling' back at her, the final product was a success...

"Well Maid" said her father-in-law " 'tis a hansom tasty pasty but 'tis a damn awful shape!".

Over time, Elaine has refined and perfected her pasty recipe, which is especially renowned for the dollop of clotted cream she adds as part of the filling.

Today, the Chough bakery employs up to 30 local people and makes over 1,000 hand made pasties a day (and that really is something to be choughed about).

The most remote pasty maker in the British Isles is Toby Tobin-Dougan. He runs the St Martins Bakery on the Isles of Scilly.

The St Martins bakery has been going for 11 years now and won UK Best Food Retailer in the BBC Radio 4 'Food and Farming' awards in 2002.The bakery makes thousands of pasties, they supply their own shop, the local pub and other outlets across the other 4 inhabited Scillonian Islands.

Toby's traditional pasties contain swede, Island potatoes, local onions and beef from Tresco. Sometimes, for those extra special occasions, he fills his pasties with all of the above as well as a dream topping of local crabmeat (which is dressed, seasoned and flavoured with their own freshly picked dill).

At the height of the season six people work at the bakery. In the summer they have to take pre-orders because they often struggle with the frantic demand.

Toby likens these holidaymaker moments to the film Zulu...Up the hill come the visitors and locals beating their carrier bags and screeching before they attack the bakery in waves. "Don't serve till you see the whites of their eyes!" is the command from the counter!

In 2010, St Martins bakery was overwhelmingly voted the best pasty-maker by the residents of the Islands. Toby insists that if you ever get the chance, the best pasty in the world is one of his and it has to be eaten while sitting on the beach at Great Bay (just round the corner and over the hill from Toby's tiny but much loved bakery).

Based on the Lizard, Ann Muller's shop Ann's Pasties can be found at the end of the yellow and black signs. Ann has lived in the area all her life and learned the art of pasty making from her mother Hettie.

"You never talk of a 'Cornish pasty' in Cornwall. It's always 'pasty', pure and simple. The second most important thing to remember when considering this savoury parcel is that a proper pasty is a meal in itself. Putting it on a plate with chips is ignorant and a sure sign that the kitchen from where it emerged spared little regard for the quality of the pasty itself. Third, it is important to note that the filling always goes into the pasty raw"

Ann's Pasties began nearly 20 years ago when she and her family took a supply of pasties to France and set up a stall at an agricultural fair in Brittany. The products proved very successful so Ann began to bake commercially. Today, Ann's Pasties employs up to 5 local people, her son runs the website and they bake and mail to order.

At the height of the summer holidays over 500 pasties are hand crimped and baked on her Lizard premises every day. Ann has served up pasties to customers from all over the world, who come, as she puts it, for a "taste of Cornwall" (yum).

When Harvey Met Warren...

Warrens is the oldest commercial bakery in Cornwall, it's a family business and they've been baking since 1860.

The business began when Miss Harvey, daughter of Mr. Harvey, the baker of St Just, met master Warren, a local farmer's son. From a pasty making point of view this was a match made in heaven.

One family provided the pastry and baked the pasties while the other family provided the filling and the rest, as they say, is history and over 150 years of history. Just a short walk from the spectacular views and harbour at Cape Cornwall; Warrens has been based in St Just for 160 years.

Their first shop opened on Queen's Street and today their large bakery is just 200 yards up the road. Warrens is an important local employer and provides over 100 jobs at their St Just bakery, a very remote and rural area. They pride themselves, as do most pasty makers in Cornwall, in sourcing the lion's share of their ingredients as locally as possible.

Malcolm Barnecutt's grandfather Percy founded the Barnecutt 'dynasty' in 1930 - it all began with a bakery in Liskeard. Percy also owned and ran a bakery in Bugle, before opening a shop and bakers in Trebetherick, still known as **Rock Bakery today** (and not just because loads of holidaymakers rock up there for their pasties!).

Percy's son, Malcolm's father Keith, opened a bakery in Padstow in the early 50s, and more shops followed in Wadebridge, St Columb and Newquay. In the late 1950s the main bakery moved from Egloshayle to Polmorla Road in Wadebridge. Which is where Malcolm learnt his trade under the expertise of his dad, and Ronald Halling, a master confectioner.

Malcolm left Polmorla Bakery in 1983 and with the invaluable support of his mother Joan Barnecutt, to whom he owes most of his success, he planned a new Bakery at Carminnow Industrial Estate, Bodmin.

On the 4th of July 1983, their first shop at the Old Guild Hall, Bodmin began trading. The fine frontage and bakers shop hides an extensive room at the rear, which was once the council chambers, but now a very pleasant restaurant, which can seat up to 100 people and is fondly known as 'Barnys'.

The shops in Bodmin, Liskeard, Launceston, Wadebridge, Rock and Boscastle have been a tremendous success and the company is now diversifying into other foodie offers including a delicatessen in St Merryn and a new idea for a café come pastry stop on the Camel Trail.

Malcolm and his son and partner James now run a thriving business employing 200 hard working staff all of whom contribute to making the "Malcolm Barnecutt Bakery" the success it is today.

8am, St Kew Highway,
I've not put a comb through my hair,
Then the smell of warm pasties,
Rises up through the air.

Up ahead in the distance,
I saw a shimmering light,
My mouth watered as I pulled in,
I had to stop for a bite.

There she stood in the doorway,
I heard the timer bell,
And I was thinking to myself,
What a wonderful story to tell.

As she opened her oven,
Of pasties baked for that day,
People lined in queues outside the door,
Just like the locals say...

Welcome to The Pasty Shop, St Kew Highway,
Such a lovely place, such a lovely place.
It's well worth the wait at Aunt Avice's, St Kew Highway.
Such a lovely taste... such a lovely taste...

(Apologies to the Eagles for the culinary adaptation of Hotel California but it I couldn't resist it)

Avice (which is Cornish for bird) has lived in the St Kew area near Wadebridge, all her life. When she met her husband-to-be, Avis had absolutely no interest in cooking whatsoever. But... as soon as she heard that his mother was a 5 star Cornish cook, Avice immediately took to the culinary arts.

After they married, both Avice and Peter took jobs on a local farm until one day when they were made redundant. That very night, Avice awoke in both a state of shock but also inspiration. She said aloud "I'm going to make pasties".

Within the next few days, Avice and her mother refined their family pasty recipe and made their first half dozen. They sold out within the first few minutes of trading. The next day they made 12, same thing happened. The next day they made 2 dozen, put a little sign up and the same thing happened.

10 years on and a thriving little business runs from a humble little shop at the service station on the outskirts of St Kew Highway (and indeed, there are queues going out the door, just like the local say).

While writing this book, I've occasionally felt like I've had a seat at what could almost be described as a scene from a pastry-based version (both short, crusted and puffed I might add!) of the Godfather trilogy (I have to thank my mate Tom for the analogy).

At 11 o'clock on a certain Thursday in the month, I'd meet with Cornwall's most prolific patrons of the pasty – a group of men and women from the finest, fastest and most formidable pastry dynasties in the West.

And whilst outside those walls, the founding committee members of the CPA may well divide and conquer - in finding new markets and clients to bake for. Within them, they talked freely and openly about their personal stories, company histories and shared very genuine passions for their number one pie.

As time went on, and the book began to emerge, it seemed to me that even the county's most prolific pasty giants had galvanised themselves around the many ingredients that make Cornwall and its pasties so incredibly special. Ironically, at the end of the project, I think we all, artisan baker, national pasty maker and local writer, agreed that despite a wonderful, and very delicious research journey, at the very heart of a pasty is a short and simple tale.

The pasty is Cornish because it had to be. Hardship and hard work kept it that way.

As modern cooking methods moved forward elsewhere, the pasty recipe, which had sustained so many Cornish for so long, had strength and support and so it stood very still. The pasties staying power and strong ties to family life and farming have woven it into the very fabric and folklore of Cornwall for centuries past and for centuries to come.

And today, whilst Cornwall might have a reputation for swanky seafood and groovy beach bars – make no mistake – the pasty is still the most popular food item on the bill. It may well have taken us that little bit longer to secure our position amongst the posh nosh of Europe but with a PGI in place, we really are cooking and so is the pasty. So...

Be sure to find one fresh from the oven,
It's a recipe that, indeed, can command and govern,
And now a stamp from Europe,
Says only Cornwall can make,
Meat, veg and history rolled in pastry and baked.

This book was bought to you by the Cornish Pasty Association and Lovely Little Books. Thanks to Mark Duddridge, Larry File, Phil Ugalde, Laura Medel and Geometry PR, Catherine Webster, Mark Muncey, Alan Adler, Jason Jobling, Paul Peace and David Rodda, Paul Colledge, Revival Design, Chris Knowles Photography, Hal Sylvester from Penryn who inspired the photographic ideas, Emma Hogg, Tom Barnecut, Margaret Dunkley and all the ladies from Lost in Song who have shared with me their pasty do's and don'ts and early childhood memories. Thanks to my parents for their continued support and thank you to all those wonderful farmers, butchers, bakers and pasty makers who take such pride in their local produce and pasties.

Everyone who has contributed to this project, especially those who belong to the Cornish Pasty Association, would like to see this text, just like the pasty recipe, evolve and grow. We'd like to hear from anyone and everyone who can share even more facts, memories or anecdotes and the flavours of Cornish life which have led to this dish over. We'd love to include them in the next serving of this book - so please get in touch.

Emma Mansfield
Lovely Little Books
c/o The Beeches
49 St Nicholas Street
Bodmin PL31 1AF

Cornish Pasty Association
c/o David Rodda
The Old Dry,
South Wheal Crofty,
Station Road,
Pool, TR15 3QG

Cornish Pasty Association
Media Enquiries
Laura Medel
Geometry PR
3 Portwall Lane
Bristol BS1 6NB

Bibliography and References

A Taste of Cornwall. Edited by Ann Butcher and Kenneth Fraser Annand. Tredinnick Press, 1994.

Arthurian Romances. Chretien de Troyes. Penguin Classics. 2004

Cornish Place Names and Language. Craig Weatherhill. Stigma Leisure 2007.

Cornish Saints and Sinners. J Henry Harris. Wildside Books, First published in 1906.

Cornish Treats. Mary Wright 1986

Cornwall and its People. A.K. Hamilton Jenkin, David and Charles 1983.

Cornwall Forever. Edited by Philip Payton. Cornwall Heritage Trust 2000.

Cornwall's Mining Heritage. Peter Stanier. Twelvehead Press, 2010.

Cornwall's Legacy to Mining. Part III. Angus Murdoch. 1970.

Gentlemens Relish. Package by Susanna Geoghegen, National Trust, 2007.

Good Things in England. Edited by Florence White. Johnathan Cape, 1932.

Pasties and Cream. Hettie Merrick. Truran Books 2005.

Pasties. Lindsey Bareham. Mabecron Books, 2008.

Pie Society. Tom Bridge, Palatine 2010.

The Canterbury Tales, Geoffrey Chaucer. Translated by Nevill Coghill. Penguin 2003.

The Chough Bakery. Elaine Ead. The Chough Bakery 2005.

The Complete Works of Shakespeare – The Alexander Text.
Edited by Peter Alexander. Collins 1989.

The Cornish Pasty. Stephen Hall. Agre Books 2001.

The Cornish Recipe Book. Edith Martin. Womens Institute. 1929.

The Official Encyclopaedia of the Cornish Pasty. Les Merton, Palores 2003.

The Pasty Book. Hettie Merrick. Tormark,1995.

The Taste of American Place. Edited by Barbara & James Shortright. Rowan & Littlefield 1998.

Topography of Great Britain / British Travellers Pocket Directory. G.A. Cook. London/ C1805.

Bibliography and References continued

The Diary of Samuel Pepys. The Pepys Library. http://www.magd.cam.ac.uk/pepys/collection.

he Cornish Pasty and Pastypedia. www.cornishpasties.org.uk

Prue Leith, Cookery Editor. How to Make A Good Cornish Pasty, The Guardian, 25th May 1984.

Colin Luckhurst. A Country Diary. The Guardian, 11th May 1984.

Antony Worrall Thompson. Food File The Daily Express, January 2001.

Valerie Elliot. Cornish pastiche facing curbs as pasties win backing to be on Europe's authentic menu. The Times. July 26 2008.

Photo credits.

Special thanks to the Cornish Studies Library, Chris Bond and Warrens for additional archive photography.

Baker, Tamar Foods. Open pasty, Crantock Bakery. Giant Pasty, The Proper Cornish Food Co. Pastyman, Phil Monckton. Tin Mine, Mark Castro. Moon Tibi Vesselenyl. Emigration Poster, Cornish Studies Library. Cornish Flag Stephen Aaron Rees. Pasty Close Up, Chris Knowles. Two men and pasty, Warrens. Pasty and Candles, Chris Knowles. Unbaked pasty, Emma Mansfield. Rough Shooter, Pedro Jorge Henriques Montiero. Pasty Recipe, Cornish Studies Library. Tywarnhayle Mine, Stephen Aaron Rees. Men looking at Potatoes, Miners eating crib, courtesy of the Proper Cornish Food Company. Pasty light bulb, Chris Knowles. Garden labourer, Proper Cornish Food Company. Crib time, St Mabyn Parish. Young boys. Cornish Studies Library. Hot Water Pasty, Chris Knowles. Danger Sign CSLD. Pachuca, Gregory Kubatyan. Cornish beach, John Williams. Geevor, Joe Gough. The Hounds of Geevor, David Kemp. Cornish Blue, Cornish Blue. Pasty Purse and Pasty with tape measure, Chris Knowles. Pile of Pasties, Proper Cornish. Flour, Mazzzur. Pasty on Plate, Crantock Bakery. Tom the potato farmer, The Proper Cornish Food Company. Swede Arnauld Weisser. Open Pasty, Crantock Bakery. Bikes and onions, The Proper Cornish Food Company. Crimping, St Martins Bakery. Crimpers, Tamar Foods. Tunnel, Geevor Tin Mine. Offering, Crantock Bakery. Postcard, Chris Bond. Cock and Hen, Crantock Bakery. Cloame Oven, Cornish Studies Library. Aga, AGA. Cornish Range, JL Engineering. Hermione Hogg, Tim and Emma Hogg. Gordon Littleton, Margaret Dunkley. Pasty at Twickenham, Phil Monckton. Pasty Appreciation t-shirt, Balcony Shirts. Mullion Cove, Stephen Aaron Res. Harvey and Co, Warrens. Tregirls Beach, Chris Sargent. Ginsters, Ginsters. Crantock, Janet Quantrill. Bodmin Moor, Martin Fowler. Lostwithiel, Paul Colledge. St Martins, Stephen Aaron Rees. Polzeath, Tim Ackroyd. Cornish Flag, Stephen Aaron Rees. Christ Pritchard, the happy pasty man, Chris Knowles. Pasty sandcastle, Phil Monckton.

If you are looking for a proper pasty, here is a list of all the members of the Cornish Pasty Association

Aunt Avice's Pasty Shop Unit 1, St Kew Service Station, St Kew Highway, PL30 3ED.

Aunty Mays, 3 The Coombe, Newlyn, Penzance, TR18 5HS.

Baker Hatt Pasty Shop, Greendale, Ellbridge Lane, Hatt, PL12 6PU.

Barnett Fare, 5a Normandy Way, Bodmin, PL31 1EX.

Berryman's Bakery, Penandrea, Redruth, TR15 2EE.

Blakes, The Master Bakers, 5 Dean Street, Liskeard, PL14 4AA.

Bridge House B+B, 4 Alexandra Terrace, Well Park Road, Drakewalls, Gunnislake, PL18 9DT.

Chapel Bakery, St Keyne, Liskeard, PL14 4SG.

Cornish Country Meats, Treverbyn Mill, Liskeard, PL14 6HG.

King's Pipe Pasties, Custom House Quay, Falmouth, TR11 3LH.

Cornish Pasty Co Mobile, Barlendew, Quintrill Downs, Newquay, TR8 4LJ.

Cornish Premier Pasties, 4 Hurling Way, St Columb Major Business Park, St Columb Major, TR9 6SX.

Crantock Bakery Ltd, Unit 2 Lodge Way, Indian Queens Ind Est, St Columb, TR9 6TF.

Crib Box Cornish Pasties, 5 Mount Charles Road, St Austell, PL25 3SB.

Dashers Cornish Bakery, 63 Fore Street, Torpoint, PL11 2AB.

Ginsters, Tavistock Road, Callington, PL17 7XG.

Greg's Bakery, The Bakery, 4 The Square, Portscatho, Truro, TR2 5HW.

Hampson of Hayle, 20 Chapel Terrace, Hayle, TR27 4AB.

Jaspers Quality Foods, Treburley, Launceston, PL15 9PU.

Jessie's Dairy, 11 Fore Street, Mousehole, Penzance, TR19 6TQ.

Lansdowne Bakery, 16 Lansdowne Road, Bude, EX23 8BH.

Lavender Delicatessen, 6a Alverton Street, Penzance, TR18 2QW.

Lostwithiel Bakery, 15 Liskerrett Road, St Martins Meadow, Liskeard.

Morris Pasties, The Pasty Shoppe Ltd, 69 Fore Street, St Columb Major, TR9 6AJ.

Nile's Bakery, The Bakery, Morven Trading Estate, St Austell, PL25 4PP.

Parkers Bakery, 2 Southgate Place, Madford Lane, Launceston, PL15 9DX.

Pasty Line, Unit 10 Water-ma-Trout Ind Est. Helston, TR13 0LW.

Pasty Shak, Unit 14 Longstone Business Park, Windsor Lane, Saltash, PL12 6DS.

Pearns Pasties of Par, 13 Harbour Road, Par, PL24 2BD.

Pellows Family Bakers Ltd, Unit 12 Longrock Ind. Est, Penzance, TR20 8HX.

Pengenna Pasties, Highfield Road Ind. Estate, Camelford, PL32 9RA.

Phelps Bakery, Phelps Pasties, 1 East Quay, Hayle, TR27 4BJ.

Polmorla Pasties, Unit 6d Kingshill Ind Est, Bude, EX23 8QN.

Prima Foods, Wheal Rose Bakery, Scorrier, Redruth, TR16 5BX.

Proper Cornish Ltd, Western House, Lucknow Road, Bodmin, PL31 1EZ.

Purdys Bakery, Seasons, 6 Windsor Place, Liskeard, PL14 6BH.

Sarah's Pasty Shop, Fore Street, Looe, PL13 1AD.

St Agnes Bakery, Churchtown, St Agnes.

St Keverne Bakery, Treskewes Ind Estate, St Keverne, TR12 6RA.

St Martins Bakery, St Martins, Isles of Scilly, TR25 0QL.

Tamar Foods, 83 Tavistock Road, Callington, PL17 7TA.

Tavistock Bakery, Fore St, East Looe, PL13 1AD.

The Chough Bakery, 34 Dennis Road, Padstow.

The Cornish Oggy Oggy Pasty Co, 17a Alverton Street, Penzance, TR18 2QP.

The Cornish Oven Ltd, Unit 7 Barncoose Ind Est, Wilson Way, Pool, Redruth, TR15 3RQ.

The Cornish Pasty Company, Quethiock House, Ganges Close, Mylor Harbour, Falmouth, TR11 5UG.

The Pasty Line, Unit 10, Water-ma-Trout Industrial Estate, Helston.

The Pasty Shop, 6 Buller St, East Looe, PL13 1AS.

The Pasty Shop Bakery, 3a Church St, Callington, PL17 7RE.

WC Rowe, Bickland Ind Est, Falmouth, TR11 4TP.

Warrens, Bosweddon Rd, St Just Penzance, TR19 7JP.

West Cornwall Pasty Company, Holbrook, The Moors, Porthleven, Helston, TR13 8HT.

Westcountry Bakery Unit 18 & 19 Trevol Business Park, Torpoint, PL11 2TB.

"The pasty is not just a tourist attraction, it's a way of life!" Luke Watts.